FIRST
PEOPLES
of NORTH
AMERICA

THE PEOPLE AND CULTURE OF THE
CHEROKEE

CASSIE M. LAWTON
RAYMOND BIAL

Cavendish
Square

New York

Published in 2017 by Cavendish Square Publishing, LLC
243 5th Avenue, Suite 136, New York, NY 10016

Copyright © 2017 by Cavendish Square Publishing, LLC

First Edition

Website: cavendishsq.com

This publication represents the opinions and views of the author based on his or her personal experience, knowledge, and research. The information in this book serves as a general guide only. The author and publisher have used their best efforts in preparing this book and disclaim liability rising directly or indirectly from the use and application of this book.

CPSIA Compliance Information: Batch #CS16CSQ

All websites were available and accurate when this book was sent to press.

Library of Congress Cataloging-in-Publication Data

Names: Lawton, Cassie M., author. | Bial, Raymond, author.
Title: The people and culture of the Cherokee / Cassie M. Lawton and Raymond Bial.
Description: New York : Cavendish Square Publishing, 2017. | Series: First peoples of North America | Includes bibliographical references and index. | Description based on print version record and CIP data provided by publisher; resource not viewed. Identifiers: LCCN 2015045091 (print) | LCCN 2015042980 (ebook) | ISBN 9781502618870 (ebook) | ISBN 9781502618863 (library bound) Subjects: LCSH: Cherokee Indians--History--Juvenile literature. | Cherokee Indians--Social life and customs--Juvenile literature.
Classification: LCC E99.C5 (print) | LCC E99.C5 L325 2016 (ebook) | DDC 975.004/97557--dc23
LC record available at http://lccn.loc.gov/2015045091

Editorial Director: David McNamara
Editor: Kristen Susienka
Copy Editor: Rebecca Rohan
Art Director: Jeffrey Talbot
Designer: Amy Greenan
Prduction Assistant: Karol Szymczuk
Photo Research: J8 Media

Printed in the United States of America

ACKNOWLEDGMENTS

This book would not have been possible without the generous help of a number of individuals and organizations that have dedicated themselves to preserving the culture of the Cherokee Nation. We would like especially to thank everyone involved in providing materials, research, photographs, and time in helping us shape this manuscript. We would like to express our deepest appreciation to Cavendish Square Publishing for publishing this book. As always, we would like to thank our families for their shining presences in our lives.

CONTENTS

A Cherokee woman dresses in traditional garb for a powwow.

AUTHORS' NOTE

At the dawn of the twentieth century, Native Americans were thought to be a vanishing race. However, despite four hundred years of warfare, deprivation, and disease, Native Americans have persevered. Countless thousands have lost their lives, but over the course of this century and the last, the populations of Native tribes have grown tremendously. Even as America's First Peoples struggle to adapt to modern Western life, they have also kept the flame of their traditions alive—the languages, religions, stories, and the everyday ways of life. An exhilarating renaissance in Native American culture is now sweeping the continent from coast to coast.

The First Peoples of North America books depict the social and cultural life of the major nations, from the early history of Native peoples in North America to their present-day struggles for survival and dignity. Historical and contemporary photographs of traditional subjects, as well as period illustrations, are blended throughout each book so that readers may gain a sense of family life in a tipi, a hogan, or a longhouse.

No single book can comprehensively portray the intricate and varied lifeways of an entire tribe, or nation. We only hope that young people will come away with a deeper appreciation for the rich tapestry of Native American culture—both then and now—and a keen desire to learn more about these first Americans.

An illustration of
Cherokee chief
Spring Frog.

CHAPTER ONE

When the white man discovered this country, Indians were running it.

—Cherokee saying

A CULTURE BEGINS

Many thousands of years ago, the first people arrived in what is now North America. Historians think they traveled across the **Bering Strait** and scattered over the land in groups. Over the years, they formed their own ways of life, their own traditions, beliefs, and languages. One such group was the Cherokee. For centuries, the Cherokee Nation has called North America home. They have developed a culture distinct from other tribes. This is their story of triumph, hardship, and perseverance.

Of Different Tongues

About two thousand years ago, the Cherokee made their way into the blue mist of the **Great Smoky Mountains**. Like all Native Americans, the Cherokee came to North America from the frozen stretches of Siberia. Most likely, they first migrated to present-day Texas or northern Mexico and then northward to the woods around the Great Lakes. There, they warred with the Iroquois and were driven to the mountains of southern **Appalachia**. Following a woodland way of life, the Cherokee farmed and hunted. They lived in harmony with nature, gathering crab apples, grapes, cherries, hickory nuts, walnuts, and chestnuts in the woods and meadows around them. The Cherokee spoke an **Iroquoian** language and were distant ancestral relations of the Iroquois of New York and Canada. In their own language, the Cherokee call themselves **Aniyvwiya** (pronounced a-ni-yoo-wi-ya), which means "real people" or "principal people." They probably got the name "Cherokee" from the neighboring Creek tribe, whose word ***tciloki*** (pronounced chi-lo-ki) means "people of a different speech."

By the late 1700s, there were about twelve thousand men, women, and children in the Cherokee Nation. Settlers often considered the Cherokee one of the "civilized" tribes because the people eventually adopted European ways. Located in eastern Tennessee, the western Carolinas, northern Georgia, and northeastern Alabama, the Cherokee homeland was one of the last Native American strongholds east of the

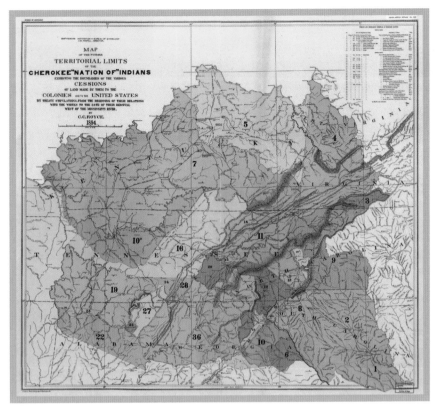

This map shows the former territorial boundaries of the Cherokee Nation.

Mississippi River. Their land included the Appalachians of the **Upland South**, with all the waters flowing down either side of the Great Smoky Mountains. White traders described them as honest, yet fierce in battle. To be clean in body and spirit, they "went to water," bathing often in clear pools and mountain streams. They considered water, the sun, and fire to be holy gifts of **Kanati**, the Great Spirit.

Connecting to the Land

The land holds great importance in Cherokee traditions. It is what gives life and sustenance. It also is the setting

The Cherokee settled near the Great Smoky Mountains some two thousand years ago.

for many Cherokee stories, beliefs, and rituals. One such story is their creation story below.

In the beginning, all creatures dwelled high in the sky, but after a time, the sky became too crowded with people and animals. Finally, the little water beetle, or Beaver's Grandchild, flew down to explore the wide ocean below the sky. The water beetle skittered this way and that over the surface of the water but could find no land. So he dived to the bottom of the ocean

The People and Culture of the Cherokee

and brought up a tiny bit of mud, which grew and grew until it became an island.

All the people and animals were eager to come to Earth, but the ground was still very soft and wet. Birds flew down to see how fast it was drying, but there was no firm place on which to land, and they became tired. Then the buzzard—who was no ordinary buzzard, but the grandfather of all buzzards—glided down to Earth. He flew very low, and his wings struck the ground, making valleys. When his wings swept upward again, he formed the Great Smoky Mountains. Worried that the entire world would become mountains and valleys, the creatures called the buzzard back to the sky, but the heart of Cherokee country remains full of mountains to this day.

When the land had dried, the people and animals came down from the sky, but the Earth was dark. The Cherokee placed the sun in a track that arched over their island, but the sun was too close and hot. The red crayfish tried to shove the sun higher in the sky, but his shell was scorched. Then the **shamans**, or priests, pushed the sun up one **handbreadth**, but it was still too hot. They moved it higher and higher until it was in just the right place under the arch of the sky—seven handbreadths high— which is why the shamans call the highest point in the sky "seventh height."

Like other Native Americans, the Cherokee lived within the natural world. They blended with the mountains, streams, and trees, like the deer, black bears, and other animals that made their home in the forests and grassy valleys called coves.

The Blue Ridge and Great Smoky Mountains where the Cherokee lived extend into present-day Tennessee and North Carolina. The ranges were named for the cool, blue haze that floats over their peaks. Pine trees jut into the sky on those high peaks, and hardwoods such as oak, hickory, sweet gum, blue ash, and dogwood blanket the slopes. The Cherokee regarded the red cedar, a fragrant wood that resists decay in damp climates, as the most sacred of trees. The mountains are also interlaced with streams, and clear water tumbles over boulders as it races down the slopes.

As the Cherokee hunted and foraged in these mountains, they always stepped lightly, paying homage to the plants and animals that sustained them.

Years passed, and the generations of Cherokee that followed the first tribes saw great changes to their land and to their livelihood. This was especially true once Europeans arrived on Cherokee territory. However, before that time, the Cherokee had developed a unique way of life. They sustained themselves on the resources around them and formed intricate beliefs, customs, and languages. In fact, according to the Cherokee Nation website www.cherokee.org, the Cherokee were hosting a thanksgiving ceremony long before the first Europeans arrived. It is called the Green

Many Native American communities celebrate the Feast of the Green Corn with dancing. This boy attends a Green Corn Ceremony in Connecticut.

Corn Ceremony and signified the start of a new year.

In time, the Cherokee would face unbelievable hardship, but through it all, they would persevere. Today, they are among the most recognizable tribes in all of North America.

The Cherokee built homes such as this one in the nineteenth century.

CHAPTER TWO

BUILDING A CIVILIZATION

The ancestors of the Cherokee first arrived on North American soil over two thousand years ago. They quickly set up communities and villages. Over time, they established a particular way of life, including their own religious practices, housing, games, tools, and government. Forming a civilization was not easy, however. It took many years and much hard work. Eventually, thousands of men, women, and children would belong to the Cherokee Nation.

Children were important members of the Cherokee Nation. Here a young Cherokee girl poses with wildflowers.

Villages

The Cherokee lived in small villages. In 1730, there were over forty villages generally clustered into four groups in the Appalachian Mountains: Valley Settlements, Overhill Settlements, Middle Settlements, and the Lower Settlements. The heart of the Cherokee Nation was in the Middle Settlements on the south bank of the Little Tennessee River in the western Carolinas. Four to six hundred people lived in each of the villages strung along valley streams and rivers. Communities were linked by seven networks of trails over which the Cherokee traveled to trade goods with the Iroquois, Chickasaw, Catawba, and other tribes as far away as the Gulf of Mexico.

Dwellings

Protected by a high log wall called a **palisade**, each town centered on the council house, a large, round, post-and-beam building with a domed roof. It was designed with seven sides so that each of the **clans** in the town—Wolf, Deer, Bird, Paint, Blue, Long Hair, and Wild Potato—could be equally close to the center. Men gathered daily in the council house, which varied in size according to the population of the town, to smoke tobacco and discuss village matters.

In each of the Cherokee towns there were seven clans, which included extended family members—not just parents, brothers, and sisters, but also aunts, uncles, cousins, and grandparents. Each clan was responsible for feeding, clothing, and sheltering its own. One did not marry into one's own clan. When a couple married, the husband typically went to live with his wife's family or in a separate home within her clan. The sections of each clan were marked off by dirt ridges, lines of stones, or rows of sticks.

Originally, the Cherokee lived in homes similar to pit houses. Dug into hillsides, these homes had log walls and a doorway on the slope. The roof was made of bark, thatch, or soil. Inside, there was a raised hearth on the dirt floor but no chimney—smoke rose through the open doorway. The walls of this cave-like dwelling were probably covered with bark or woven mats. Homes were grouped together in villages that probably also had sweat lodges, storehouses, and small buildings.

Later, the Cherokee began to construct sturdy, permanent homes with clay walls and thatched roofs.

To make these homes, they set large posts into the ground about three feet apart, with smaller poles placed between them. They wove supple branches or split canes between the posts to make walls, which they plastered with a thick coat of clay mixed with grass. Sometimes, the Cherokee whitewashed their homes with lime obtained by crushing burnt clamshells. They made the domed roofs in the same manner as the walls, then covered the woven canes with bark or thatch to shed the rain. These houses had no windows and only a small doorway covered by an animal skin or mat to keep out the cold. Inside, a basin was scooped out in the middle of the floor for the fire, and a circular hearthstone for baking bread was placed next to it. Women kept a fire burning continually, with the smoke rising through a small hole in the roof.

Cherokee houses gradually evolved into square or rectangular homes with gabled roofs. These buildings were similar in structure to contemporary homes, except that they had a post-and-beam frame, thick clay walls, and saplings lashed down on the roof to hold the shingles in place. They had one or two stories and several rooms to accommodate large families, many of whom slept in bunk beds. During the warm summer months, it is believed that the Cherokee lived in large homes with woven reed walls and a long porch across the front. After the Cherokee came into contact with English settlers in the mid-1700s, they began to build and live in log cabins.

Hothouses

During the coldest part of the winter, families stayed in a hothouse, a stout log frame built into a slope and

A Cherokee sweat lodge in North Carolina.

covered with a mound of dirt. A fire was kept burning throughout the day to warm the house, then banked at night. Since there was no smoke hole and only a small doorway, the hothouse would become too smoky if the fire was left burning at night. People slept on wide benches lining the walls, and the dwellings were so warm that bedcovers and clothes were hardly necessary.

Shamans often used their hothouses as sweat lodges for ceremonies and medical treatments. They heated river rocks in the fire and raked them out over the ground. Then they poured a liquid of steeped wild parsnip roots or bark from persimmon, mulberry, cherry, or poplar trees over the hot stones. After their sweat baths, men took a cold plunge in the river. Around the flickering orange fire of the winter homes, myth keepers recalled the sacred legends of the Cherokee past.

Furniture and Other Possessions

The Cherokee kept little furniture and only a few possessions in their homes: rugs, baskets, clay pots, stools, and beds, along with clothing and some food. They made spoons from bison horns and fashioned many articles from wood and gourds, including masks to frighten enemies. They used tobacco widely, especially in ceremonies, and they carved pipe bowls from soapstone, then fitted them with wooden stems. Placed at one end of the home, their beds had short posts for legs, with white oak or ash splints woven on a sapling frame. People slept on rush or split-cane mats on the beds, covered with skins from bears, elks, deer, or mountain lions.

Women made striking hemp-thread rugs painted with imaginative and colorful designs. They also wove baskets that were both lovely and useful for storage. Early Cherokee baskets were made from hemp fibers or the inner bark of mulberry trees. Later, strips of **river cane** and white oak were used to weave sturdy and beautiful baskets, often with a bold zigzag double weave called a lightning design. The Cherokee stored food in these baskets as well as in pots, jugs, and jars. They kept some food in the home for daily use but placed most corn, beans, and other provisions in village storehouses made of white oak, hickory, poplar, and sassafras. Raised 4 to 5 feet (1.2 to 1.5 meters) off the

Cherokee wove elaborate baskets and used them to carry items.

ground, these buildings protected the corn harvest from rodents and rain.

Cherokee women shaped pottery entirely by hand. Using a mixture of light, sandy clay and fine, dark clay dug from riverbanks, they formed coils, which they then pinched and smoothed with their fingers to make a jar or pot. Sometimes they simply used their fingers to form a cup or bowl; other times they used stones and shell scrapers to smooth the clay surface, then stamped a design on the vessel with a carved wooden paddle. The Cherokee dried their pottery for three days, then fired the pieces on a hearth of flat stones. They placed the pottery with the open mouths toward the fire for about one hour, until the clay turned slightly brown. Then, they rolled the pots and jars directly into the embers, mouth down, and covered them with dried bark, which burned away in an hour. Finally, they threw a handful of bran or broken-up corncobs into the vessel, which quickly ignited. The pottery was then turned upside down to smoke and waterproof the inside.

Leading the Community

Each town was represented by a council. The council was headed by a shaman, who had no authority but advised on spiritual and medical matters. There were two chiefs—the **White chief** (also known as "the most beloved man"), who handled daily concerns of the town, and the **Red chief**, who offered advice regarding war parties, victory dances, and the spirited games that were a vital part of the Cherokee way of life. Seven elder men were chosen from each clan. These men usually led discussions, although all Cherokee men participated. The council discussed town concerns, including religious matters, and decided by **consensus**. Cherokee society had little need of formal laws. Seeking harmony in relations with each other, they maintained order by social pressure and negotiation among disputing individuals or clans.

The Cherokee were a highly organized people, not only within each village but in the nation as a whole, with two forms of government—the White for civil or peacetime affairs and the Red for waging war. The White chief was the religious head or high priest as well. Next in importance to the chief was the right-hand man, or *itausta*, and then the chief speaker. The chief had seven councilors, including the right-hand man, who formed the main government. The Red organization consisted of a group of officials corresponding in rank to the White leaders, except that they were responsible only for military activities. The

A Cherokee woman makes a basket.

White organization had slightly more power because the Red chief was selected by the White chief.

There were other important people within Cherokee government, notably "the beloved woman," an elderly matron honored for her wisdom and goodness. Seven women, usually the eldest women in the nation, also took part in many council ceremonies.

The national government met in a large seven-sided building situated on a high mound in the capital. The capital was not fixed at first, but it was always in the village of the White chief, although **New Echota** eventually became the traditional capital. As in the

CONSTITUTION

OF THE

CHEROKEE NATION,

MADE AND ESTABLISHED

AT A

GENERAL CONVENTION OF DELEGATES,

DULY AUTHORISED FOR THAT PURPOSE.

AT

NEW ECHOTA,

JULY 26, 1827.

——————

PRINTED FOR THE CHEROKEE NATION,
AT THE OFFICE OF THE STATESMAN AND PATRIOT,
GEORGIA.

The title page of the Cherokee constitution of 1827.

town council house, the seating arrangement was highly formalized, with the White chief occupying the seat of honor. Here, Cherokee leaders held elaborate national ceremonies, assembled war parties, and administered laws.

A Growing Culture

The Cherokee lived this way for many hundreds of years. They sometimes faced challenges and confrontation from other tribes, but for the most part, their communities were well developed and thriving. By the time the first European settlers arrived in the sixteenth century, the Cherokee had formed their own civilization. All too soon their way of life would be threatened and changed in ways they could never have imagined.

A man shows his family a squirrel he shot, circa 1936.

CHAPTER THREE

Don't let yesterday use up too much of today.

—Cherokee saying

LIFE IN THE CHEROKEE NATION

Life in the Cherokee Nation differed whether you were a man, woman, or child. For the most part, men were often away on a hunt, fighting, or trading, while the women were left to raise the crops, tend gardens, and care for their children. In the Cherokee community, women wielded a great deal of power and played a central role. Interestingly, the women were the heads of the household and owned the most property in a village, even though the men led discussions and made decisions for the Cherokee community.

The Life Cycle

As with each Native American community, the Cherokee had their own beliefs, traditions, and customs. They also had their own thoughts about the different cycles of life.

Being Born

When a Cherokee woman learned that she was going to have a baby, she told her husband, who spread the good news throughout the village. He then built a special dwelling where she confined herself for the last three months of her pregnancy. She had to follow many rules and rituals; most notably, at each new moon, she was taken to water. Accompanied by her husband, mother, and a shaman, she prayed to be purified. The shaman poured water on the top of her head and chest, then he attempted to foresee the child's future.

When the woman went into labor, she might be assisted by as many as four women. However, the expectant mother usually had little difficulty in childbirth, and her mother or grandmother provided all necessary help. Sometimes a shaman might be present to pray for a quick and safe delivery, but otherwise, men were not allowed in the dwelling.

During childbirth, the woman knelt on a robe. If the newborn fell on its back, it was good, but if the baby landed on its chest, it was considered a bad sign. After birth, the newborn was immediately wrapped in a cloth, taken to a stream, and immersed until the cloth floated away to remove any ill fortune.

A Cherokee mother shows her daughter how to sew.

When the baby was one or two days old, the shaman waved it four times over a fire and offered a blessing. When the baby was either four or seven days old, the shaman took it to a stream and prayed to the Creator that it might have a long and happy life.

Then, a naming ceremony took place in which a respected, elderly woman christened the baby. Often, she selected a name based on the baby's resemblance to an object, something that had happened at the birth, or a unique trait of the child. Later, the child might be renamed because of a heroic deed, such as killing a bear. Names gave special identity to the child and could never be misused. If a shaman's cures failed during treatment of an illness, he concluded that the patient's name was no longer effective. He then took the patient to water and gave him or her a new name.

The Cherokee often bathed in waters such as these to keep the body and soul clean.

Growing Up

For the first two years, the child was bathed daily in the river. At age four or five, the father or a mother's brother took charge of the boys, who were taught hunting, fighting, and other ways of the men. A few boys, who came to be called "devoted sons," were encouraged to become shamans when they grew up. Girls learned the roles of women by helping their mothers and older sisters in the home and fields.

Mothers and fathers loved and indulged their children, for which they were criticized by settlers. Yet children honored and respected their parents, as well as the elderly people of the village.

A young woman having her first menstrual period went to a separate camp, away from her family. No one was allowed to touch her. She could not even handle her own food, and another woman had to feed her. After seven days, to purify herself, she bathed and washed her clothing as well as anything else she had touched. She then returned to her clan, and if she wished, she could marry a young man in the village.

Marrying

A woman and man from different clans could freely choose to marry each other, and husbands and wives decided together where they wanted to live. The house in which they lived, however, belonged to the wife, as did the children, who were raised by her and taught by her brothers. Since the man married into the woman's

This illustration from the 1500s shows a Native American man and woman eating together.

clan, he was considered an outsider, but his children became part of the clan.

Cherokee families were matrilineal, meaning children traced their names and family history through their mothers. Even if children had a white father, they were full members of the nation and the clan, as long as their mother was Cherokee.

There were strict laws against marrying anyone from one's own clan. At one time, the penalty for this offense was death; later, whipping became the punishment. Typically, when a young man wished to marry a young woman from another clan, he spoke with his parents, then asked the consent of her parents. He might also speak with a brother from each of the clans. If everyone agreed, a date was set, and the shaman was informed of the marriage plans.

On the morning of the wedding, the shaman laid two roots in the palm of his hand. Facing east, he prayed for the couple. If the roots did not move or if one root withered, it was believed the couple would not live well together. If the roots moved together, it was a good sign, and the marriage took place.

Dying

When a person, especially an elderly father, was about to die, he gathered his children around him. He offered advice about their futures and reminded them of Cherokee customs. Young children were then sent away because only the shaman and adult relatives were allowed to be present at the deathbed.

Women wept profusely, and at the moment of death, they cried out, repeating the name of the deceased

The Cherokee respected all members of their tribe, young and old alike.

over and over. During seven days of mourning, men seldom cried, but they smeared ashes on their heads and put on worn clothing.

A relative closed the deceased's eyelids and washed the body. Soon after the death, a shaman who was responsible for burials arrived at the home. He buried the loved one in the dirt floor beneath the place of death, under the hearth, or just outside the dwelling. A distinguished chief was buried under his seat in the council house. Belongings were either buried with the deceased or burned at the gravesite.

Everyone in the deceased's household was now considered unclean, and furnishings, clothing, and food had to be thrown away. The shaman then ritually purified the house. He thoroughly cleaned the hearth and kindled a new fire. Over this fire he brewed a pot of tea made from a special weed. The family members drank this tea and washed themselves with it. To cleanse the house further, the shaman smoked a pipe and built a fire with cedar boughs and another special weed. He then hid what was left of the purifying ritual in a hollow tree.

Lastly, he took the family members to a stream and prayed over them as they strode into the water. They allowed their garments to be carried away with the current, and when they came out of the water, they put on new clothing.

When the mourners returned to their purified home, the shaman gave them a string of beads to ease their grief and a piece of tobacco to "enlighten their eyes," so they could bravely look to the future.

The Cherokee had a strong belief that after a person died, his or her soul came back as a ghost. The ghost could appear at any time and in any place. Some, but not all, people could see the ghost. Today, many still hold this belief.

Crops and Clothes

Against a backdrop of hazy blue mountains, Cherokee women farmed the rich soil of coves, or valleys. Their primary crops were corn, beans, pumpkins, squash, sunflowers, and tobacco. Cherokee mothers and daughters grew three different kinds of corn for roasting, boiling, and grinding into meal for bread. Fields and gardens were owned by the entire clan. Each woman helped to raise and harvest the precious yellow grain, which was stored in a common building. No one hoarded food; everyone took only as much corn as they needed to feed their family. The Cherokee were a generous people who believed in equality and sharing among themselves. Each year they held ceremonies in which they destroyed possessions to show how little their property mattered to them.

Cherokee women prepared all the meals and taught their daughters how to cook and manage their

Corn is ground up using a mortar and pestle.

home life. They fried, roasted, or boiled various dishes that were so delicious they are still eaten today. The Cherokee ate fish and meat, primarily deer, rabbit, squirrel, and turkey, along with beans, squash, and corn. A typical meal might include warm boiled beans with bread made from a bean and corn batter that was wrapped in cornhusks and baked over hot coals. Corn, often in the form of parched cornmeal, was the most important food. It was prepared in different ways and included in many dishes. To parch corn, women cooked a mixture of cornmeal and wood ashes in a pot over an open fire. **Parched corn** kept well on long hunting trips and was used in a variety of foods, such as swamp potatoes, stewed groundhog, and wild grape soup.

The Cherokee made some very interesting dishes, including yellow jacket soup, chestnut bread, hickory

RECIPE

CORN AND BEANS

INGREDIENTS

Indian corn (large white); may substitute
    16-ounce (540-milliliter) can of hominy corn

Colored beans; may substitute 16-ounce can (540 mL)
    of kidney beans

Molasses to taste

The Cherokee usually removed the "skin" of the kernels with lye to make hominy, then cooked it together with colored beans in an iron pot. Sometimes they added pumpkin or a mixture of cornmeal, beaten walnuts, and hickory nuts, and sometimes they added molasses as a sweetener. They either ate this dish fresh or after it began to sour.

    In your recipe, drain hominy corn and kidney beans. Place in a cooking pot and add enough water to cover the mixture. Simmer for 10 minutes. Sweeten with a little molasses or maple syrup.

nut soup, "slick-go-downs" (mushrooms), cornbread baked on bark, "leather breeches" (green beans), and "knee-deeps" (small frogs). They drank spicewood tea, "possum grape drink," and "parched corn drink."

Cherokee women either grew or gathered what they needed to feed their families. In addition to basic foods, maple syrup was boiled down in the spring to make crumbly sugar; powdered honey locust pods were also used as a sweetener.

Myths, magic, and legends permeated Cherokee life, even in the preparation of meals. To hurry the cooking of food, women sometimes recited the following charm about the red crayfish, a small creature that cooks rapidly: "Now! Ha! Now very quickly I have just come to put the Red Crayfish in the pot!"

To make clothing, women tanned the hides of deer, beavers, mountain lions, otters, and other

Baskets were important and useful items to the Cherokee people.

animals, although they mostly used **buckskin** from tanned deerskins. With fishbone needles, they sewed wraparound skirts for their daughters and themselves. During cold weather, they also wore capes of bison calfskin with the hair turned inside. Later, they adorned cloth skirts with rows of brass beads or leather belts fastened with buckles. Men and boys wore **breechcloths** made from a piece of buckskin drawn up between their legs and around their waists. In summer they also sometimes wore buckskin shirts but most often went bare-chested. In winter, their shirts were made from the skin of bears, beavers, otters, and panthers, with the fur on the inside for greater warmth. Around the villages, everyone either went barefoot or, during cold weather, wore soft deerskin moccasins. When hunting, men wore tall deerskin boots fringed with fawns' hooves or turkey feet.

The Cherokee often decorated their clothing. Women spun possum fur into threads that they dyed red, yellow, or dark brown. To make black threads, they spun bear fur. These colored threads were woven into the caps, belts, and garters with which the Cherokee adorned themselves. Men sometimes wore capes or mantles made from buckskin or turkey and eagle feathers. Prominent warriors wore bands of otter skin on their heads, upper arms, and just below their knees. The chiefs' robes were often quite elaborate—made of white or yellow leather decorated with crane feathers or strings of deer hooves, with sleeves of raccoon fur. Chiefs' headdresses were often made from a roll of raccoon skins dyed yellow or, for the peace chief, from white crane feathers.

Dennis Wolfe, a full-blooded Cherokee, wears ceremonial clothes.

Warfare, Trade, and Fun

When boys grew up, their days were filled with warfare, trading, ball games, and hunting and fishing. During the coldest half of the year, Cherokee warriors patrolled their land, engaging in bloody skirmishes to drive back the Creek, Chickasaw, Catawba, and other tribes that tried to encroach upon the mountains. The Cherokee also made raids on lands claimed by other tribes. Sometimes they sold captured enemies as slaves. If one of their warriors was slain, they sought vengeance. His spirit would not rest until the murderer himself was killed.

Cherokee men were active traders. They traded silver ornaments they had crafted, as well as deerskins and beaver pelts, with other tribes, and eventually with European traders. A man could become wealthy, but if he did, he had to deal with the disapproval of others in the clan and town who were not as well off. People might scorn his wealth, and the shamans might wish him ill.

Like other eastern tribes, the Cherokee played a ball game similar to **lacrosse**. Called "the friend or companion of battle," or simply "little brother of war," these stickball games were very rough—players often suffered broken bones, torn muscles, cuts, and bruises. Elaborate rituals preceded the game. If someone wanted a contest, he gathered his friends and sent a challenge to another town. If the town accepted the challenge, people were selected for various tasks: an elderly man to oversee the game, a person to sing for the players, another to whoop, and a musician for seven women who danced on the seventh night of preparations for the game.

The night before the game, players danced together around the fire with their ball sticks, pretending that they were playing. Then they hung up their sticks, went to a brisk stream, and bathed seven times, after which they went to bed. At daybreak, the shaman took them to the creek again. During their preparations the players were not allowed to go near women, and they could not eat meat or anything hot or salty. Seven women were chosen to prepare meals of cold bread and a drink of parched cornmeal and water. The men could not be served by women, so boys brought the food to them. During the day the men were scratched with rattlesnake fangs or turkey quills to toughen them for the "little brother of war."

The two teams gathered on a large field where goalposts were set up at each end. Players paired off, the referee threw the ball up in the air between the two captains, and a mad scramble ensued. The game was "anything goes," and there was biting, gouging, choking, scratching, twisting arms and legs, and banging each other with the wooden rackets. The object of the game was to carry the ball between the goals twelve times. The first team with twelve wooden pegs stuck in the ground by the shaman won the game. There was no time limit, and often the game went on until dark. There was also no time-out or substitution. If a player was injured, he and the opponent with whom he was paired both left the game. Cherokee gathered from throughout the mountains to watch and bet on these hotly contested games.

When they weren't trading, fighting, or playing ball games, men hunted for animals, which provided clothing as well as food for the village. Women cured, or tanned, deer hides into supple buckskin. The Cherokee stalked bears, deer, and elks with bows and arrows, and hunters wore deerskins complete with antlers to disguise themselves. They killed rabbits, squirrels, turkeys, and other small game with blowguns and darts. Skilled hunters blew the feathered darts through long hollowed-out canes with remarkable accuracy.

Expert fishermen, the Cherokee used spears, bows and arrows, and hooks and lines to catch trout and catfish in the clear streams splashing down the mountainsides. Sometimes they fished from canoes made from hollowed-out logs. They also made clever wooden traps and baskets, which they dipped like nets into the water. Other times they dammed a stream and threw mashed chestnuts into the water to stun the fish. The Cherokee then easily collected by hand as many fish as they needed. When they broke up the dam, the rest of the fish recovered and swam away.

Forming a Lifestyle

All of this helped the Cherokee form a unique lifestyle. Some of the traditions and cultural practices have changed, but many others have persisted through the centuries, even during especially difficult times. Today, the Cherokee remember and celebrate the culture of their ancestors, keeping their identity as a tribe alive and at the forefront of their minds.

Darts like these were used to teach young boys how to hunt.

This woman uses brightly colored beads to decorate a belt.

CHAPTER FOUR

May your moccasins make happy tracks in many snows, and may the Rainbow always touch your shoulder.

—Cherokee blessing

BELIEFS OF THE CHEROKEE

As with many Native American tribes, the Cherokee held their own religious and tribal beliefs and customs. Many of these traditions remain important to the Cherokee today. There were rituals, ceremonies, and stories devoted to every aspect of life. In the present day, Cherokee men, women, and children celebrate the stories of their ancestors.

Many beliefs, particularly stories passed down over generations, are considered sacred and are deeply rooted in the Cherokee Nation's way of life.

The Art of Hunting

In the early days, the men in the clan taught the boys how to hunt, fish, and fight. Most notably, a boy's mother's brothers were often his teachers, although sometimes all the young men in a town were instructed together. Boys were both praised and chided, but never struck, which was a sign of disrespect. They were allowed only two meals a day to instill a good appetite and willpower.

A young hunter first had to learn the ways of the animals—to become one with them by entering their habitat. Sometimes he was left by a stream to study the animals that came to drink at the water's edge, or he was sent high up a mountain, where he learned to hide in the green leaves and shadows. During his training as a hunter, he went all day without food to learn discipline. He was taught to be as silent as his own breath, from daybreak to dusk, neither speaking nor making a sound, so that he could better listen to the voices of the woods. Hunting was a way of life, and a boy learned not to change nature but to find a place for himself within it. Later, if a young man wished to become a shaman, he could be apprenticed, but only after he had learned to be a good hunter and warrior.

The young hunter learned that because people had wastefully killed too much game in the past, the animals had cursed them with disease. Certain plants, known only to the shamans, provided cures. A young man

Hunters used knives like this to kill or injure their prey.

believed that if he sprinkled tobacco on a heap of ashes at home and it caught fire, he would have a good hunt. If the tobacco did not ignite, he would find no game. A hunter knew not to kill the wolf, which was considered a messenger from the spirit world. One could sit by the fire at night, listen to the wolves' distant, mournful howls, and learn much. If a hunter killed a wolf, game would vanish, and his bow would become useless until purified by the shaman. The hunter could also place the weapon in a swift river overnight or give it to a child to play with as a toy for a while. Yet he had to remember that the wolf always sought revenge—death for death. The young hunter could protect himself by reciting a prayer and bathing morning and evening in a stream.

Entertaining the Children

As they grew up, children were praised and entertained; they were given furry toys and allowed to have pets. They were also thrilled by stories about the imaginary little people who inhabited the land around them. Called **yûñwi tsunsdi**, the little people were Cherokee—they spoke Cherokee and ate corn, beans, and game. Just 1 to 3 feet (0.3 to 1 meters) tall, the little men had long gray hair and beards and often wore hats of several colors. The little women, who looked and dressed like the Cherokee, were lovely and delicate. They danced at celebrations and sat long hours in the council house, telling stories and discussing important matters of the day.

Where were the little people? They were hiding in the bushes, parents told their children, or behind the misty veil of a waterfall. They were everywhere, possibly behind the nearest tree, but they could not be seen. Most often, they were heard in the songs of birds or the crash of thunder. The little people were often kind, helping young Cherokee when they were lost—they knew all the paths in the woods. They were good company for lonely people, and when a grandmother died they showed her the way to the Great Spirit. If children ever saw a little person, they were not to tell anyone for seven days or bad luck would befall them. However, the little people were not always helpful. When rocks tumbled down a hillside, one could be sure the little people were up there giggling at their mischief.

Religious Beliefs

The religion of the Cherokee people was not based on the idea of a separate god. Instead, they felt a divine presence in everything around them—animals, plants, ground, wind, and sky. They saw themselves living in a world between the earth and sky. To them, all things in nature were equal to humans, and they respected the environment. The spirit of nature was also reflected in their legends. Many of these, such as "How the Milky Way Came To Be," "The First Fire," and "The Origin of Strawberries," dealt with the beginning of things in nature. Other stories, such as "Why the Mink Smells," "Why the Buzzard's Head Is Bare," and "The Rattlesnake's Vengeance," explained the ways of certain animals, sometimes in a humorous manner.

Here is a legend about the possum, which tells how its tail came to be bare. The story is also a lighthearted lesson about the consequence of being too vain:

> Long ago, Possum had a long, bushy tail. He was so proud of it that he brushed it every day and sang about it every night. He bragged about it so much that Rabbit, whose tail had been pulled off by Bear, became jealous and decided to play a trick on Possum.
>
> There was to be a great council meeting and dance for all the animals. Possum agreed to come, but only if he was to be given a seat of honor. "I have such a handsome tail I should sit where everyone can see me," he explained.

Today, Cherokee territory has changed from what it once was centuries ago.

Rabbit agreed and even offered to send Cricket to comb his tail.

In the morning, Cricket went to Possum's house to get him ready for the dance. Possum stretched himself out and shut his eyes while Cricket combed his tail and wrapped a string around it to keep it smooth. But all the while, Cricket was clipping off the hair to the roots.

That night Possum went to the dance and found the best seat ready for him, just as Rabbit had promised. When it was his turn to dance he loosened the red string and stepped

The People and Culture of the Cherokee

onto the floor. "See my beautiful tail," he sang. Everyone shouted as he danced. "See what a pretty color it has," he bragged. "See how bushy it is!" The other animals shouted more loudly, and Possum was delighted. "See how my tail sweeps the ground." Then he noticed that the animals were laughing—and at him! He looked down at his tail and saw that there wasn't a hair left—it was as bare as a lizard's tail! He was so astonished that he couldn't say a word. He rolled helpless on the ground, feet in the air, and grinned, just as the possum does to this day when taken by surprise.

Rituals and Dancing

Over the course of the year, the Cherokee held several great festivals, either in the council house or at a sacred place called the **square ground** or **dance ground**. An opening in the forest canopy, the square ground was surrounded by rows of log seats under sloped roofs, with a bushy-topped tree rising from the very center. Ceremonies held there related to the seasons and the Cherokee's religious beliefs. Among these were the first new moon of spring, green corn (a time of thanksgiving and renewal in which people gave thanks to the corn spirit for an abundant harvest), October new moon, and renewal of brotherhood (also called reconciliation) ceremonies.

As part of these seasonal events, the Cherokee held many lively dances in which water drums, gourd rattles, and turtle shell rattles were used as musical

Actors perform a Cherokee dance during "Unto These Hills" in 2006.

The People and Culture of the Cherokee

instruments. In the **uka** dance, the chief, or uka, himself offered thanksgiving in a spirit of rejoicing. Two persons were especially important in dances: the leader, who preserved order and made sure the dance was carried out properly, and the lead singer. The green corn dance was originally part of the Green Corn Ceremony, which celebrated the first harvest. This was one of the most important festivals of the Cherokee year. The warrior dance was performed before men went to war. There were also friendship dances, in which both men and women participated. Women danced either with their husbands or, if they were single, with their brothers

This illustration shows men and women celebrating the Green Corn Ceremony.

or a young man from their clan. The round dance, or **atayohi**, was a special dance that concluded all-night sessions of dancing. Led by a woman wearing leg rattles, the women danced counterclockwise to four songs. As the songs became faster, the men paired off with the women. The Cherokee also danced whenever they wished to celebrate a good hunt or other joyful event.

The owl is sacred to the Cherokee people.

Sacred Animals

The Cherokee considered many animals sacred. Two of the most sacred animals were the cougar and the owl. According to some versions of the Cherokee creation story, these animals stayed awake for all seven days of the creation, and were the only ones to do so. Thus, they were viewed as possessing immense power. Today, cougars and owls still hold a special place in Cherokee tradition.

The Cherokee also believed that the eagle had magical powers, and the eagle dance (also called the victory dance) was very important to their way of life. The eagle dance was performed when one of the great birds was killed for its feathers, to welcome the spirit of the eagle to the village.

Divided into three parts, the dance celebrated victory and honored the eagle for giving its feathers. Dancers either carried a feather wand and a rattle in each hand or a wand in both hands and danced to the beat of turtle shell rattles and water drums. Since the eagle and rattlesnake were believed to be deadly enemies, the dance was held only in the winter when the snake was asleep. If the rattlesnake heard the dancing and singing, it would become more deadly. Other accounts say the dance was not held in the summer because it would bring on an early frost.

Women joined in the eagle dance. They danced with feather wands, and a lead woman wore turtle shell rattles strapped to her knees. Participants formed two

The cougar is among the most sacred animals to the Cherokee Nation.

rings, the women in an inner circle, and they danced around a tree in the center of the square ground, waving the wands as they moved. There were different sets of songs and a variety of steps. It was critically important that the dancers not drop their wands or even allow them to touch the ground. It was believed that anyone who did so would soon die.

The Effect of European Arrival

In the early 1700s, the first European settlers arrived in Cherokee territory. They brought with them many new customs and traditions, as well as a new religion: Christianity.

At first, the Cherokee were curious about these newcomers. They offered them advice on what crops to grow, traded with them, and showed them where to find animals to hunt. Over time, missionaries also arrived. These men and women sought to change the Cherokee's way of life by converting them to Christianity. Some Cherokees did accept Christianity and eventually built churches. Others, however, refused to forsake their religion. They resisted efforts to change their lifestyle and beliefs, but over time, many Cherokee villages began to accept more European building techniques and practices.

European influence on the Cherokee way of life would continue into the nineteenth century. As more people moved into territory once cared for by the Cherokee, the Cherokee began to lose their land. This process reached intensity in the mid-1800s with the Indian Removal Act, which would force the Cherokee out of their homeland for good. The Cherokee were

This nineteenth-century illustration shows a European named Sir Alexander Cuming venturing to meet the Cherokees in South Carolina, circa 1730.

relocated to Oklahoma on a journey history refers to as the Trail of Tears.

Despite the hardships they faced, the Cherokee continued to persevere. They celebrated their beliefs and traditions and remembered the ways of their ancestors. Today, many Cherokee men, women, and children uplift the memories of their ancestors and celebrate their customs.

With the arrival of Europeans, the way of life for many Native American communities began to change.

CHAPTER FIVE

The trail of exiles was a trail of death.

—Private John G. Burnett regarding the Cherokee Indian Removal, 1838–1839

OVERCOMING HARDSHIPS

The history of Cherokee encounters with Europeans stretches back to the 1500s. It is believed that Spanish explorer Hernando de Soto encountered members of the Cherokee Nation in 1540 on his expedition. Decades later, the Cherokee met the French. These men were traders, who arrived in Cherokee country to trap animals and trade. While Europeans influenced some Cherokee practices, it was not until English settlers built the settlement of Jamestown, Virginia, that the Cherokee's way of life truly began to change.

A Changing World

The Cherokee found themselves caught between British and the French settlers. Both groups were invading the Cherokee's mountain home and establishing their presence in Cherokee territory. They played one against the other until the French left North America following the French and Indian War (1754–1763). After this, the Cherokee were at the mercy of the British.

Before this, however, the settlers had affected Cherokee life in other ways. The Cherokee population was devastated by smallpox epidemics in 1738 and 1750—just as settlers were pushing into the mountains. Warriors tried to keep the settlers away, but there was a never-ending wave of them. "You will find the settlement of this land dark and bloody," Dragging Canoe, a great chief, said at the time.

Several Cherokee towns joined the British in fighting the settlers during the Revolutionary War (1775–1783). When the American colonies won their independence, the Cherokee found it more difficult to defend their ancestral home. "Whole nations have melted away like balls of snow before the sun," said Dragging Canoe in an address to the Cherokee council in 1775.

The Cherokee signed several treaties with the United States in which they agreed to give up some parts of their homeland if they were allowed to keep others. Yet their conflict with the newcomers became as much a cultural struggle as a war for land. How could they match the technology of rifles and gunpowder? The settlers also had metals—iron, silver, and lead— along with the knowledge and skill to fashion useful

The People and Culture of the Cherokee

This engraving shows Cherokee chiefs from Carolina, circa 1730.

tools. They farmed the land efficiently and made good, warm clothing as well as other household articles. White people also had a written language and mathematics, and they had their own music—the Cherokee were amazed that such a beautiful sound could issue from an odd-shaped box like the fiddle.

The Cherokee wanted European goods and knowledge. In exchange, they sold beaver pelts. When these became scarce, they sold Creek captives as slaves, and then they sold their land. As Christian missionaries converted people and white traders married Native women, the Cherokee began to adopt European ways of life, including clothing, household goods, and housing. Like some settlers, they farmed the land, and a few even owned African-American slaves. George Washington furnished the Cherokee with spinning wheels and cottonseeds, and women made clothes from the cotton they grew in their fields. Shamans argued against these European influences because they feared that the Cherokee would lose their identity as a people.

Preserving the Language

In 1809, a mixed-blood Cherokee named Sequoyah, also known as George Gist and George Guess, began a twelve-year project in which he invented a Cherokee syllabary, a kind of alphabet, so the tribe would have a written language. The alphabet, which Sequoyah called "talking leaves," consisted of eighty-five characters representing each of the different sounds in the Cherokee language. Sequoyah was the only person in history to create an alphabet entirely on his own. With the written language, the Cherokee were able to operate a printing press with which they published their own constitution and a newspaper, started in 1828, called the *Cherokee Phoenix*.

The Cherokee language is quite fascinating, but it can also be challenging for non-Native speakers. It does not have several consonants found in English and contains a few sounds not commonly found in Western languages. There are also several dialects—two in Tennessee and the Carolinas, and a separate Oklahoma Cherokee that is a blend of several dialects spoken by those who migrated west. The Cherokee language relies heavily on subtle changes of pitch or tone,

Sequoyah brought a written language to the Cherokee people.

which are sometimes difficult to translate to the Roman alphabet. To help you pronounce Cherokee words, here is a list of vowels and consonants, along with their sounds. The examples are based on the *Cherokee-English Dictionary* published by the Oklahoma Cherokee, formally known as the Cherokee Nation.

The Cherokee Nation website has a page dedicated to the tribe's language. To learn more, see: www.cherokee.org/AboutTheNation/Language.aspx.

a	as in f*a*ther
e	as in *e*cho
i	as in s*i*t
o	as in h*e*llo
u	as in r*u*le
v	as in c*u*t

The letter *v* represents a vowel that is similar to the *u* in "cut," but with a deeper nasal sound. Cherokee vowels may be long or short. Most often, vowels at the end of a syllable are relatively long. Vowels in the middle of syllables are short.

Consonants are generally pronounced as in English, except that *g* is always hard, as in "go." There are no sounds in the Cherokee language for the consonants *b*, *p*, or *z*. The question mark (?) is used for a sound known as the glottal stop that is common to many Native American languages. Like a short breath or catch in the throat, it is similar to the sound between the first and second "oh" in "oh-oh," or the sound in place of the *t* in the Cockney pronunciation of "bottle."

Here are some examples of everyday words that you might say in Cherokee.

Common Words and Phrases

gule	acorn
achuja	boy

udo	brother
wesa	cat
ayohli	child
selu	corn
koga	crow
ahawi	deer
gihli	dog
elohi	earth
edoda	father
aja?di	fish
inage?i	forest
unali?i	friend
walosi	frog
agehyuja	girl
osiyo, siyo	hello (two versions)
juwenvsv?i	home
gahljode	house
nvda	moon
uji	mother
odalv?i	mountain
hla	no
jisdu	rabbit
uweyv?i	river
udo	sister
saloli	squirrel
nvdo	sun

wado	thank you
ukedaliyv?i	valley
ama	water
vv	yes

The words for sun and moon are the same. They are distinguished by adding a second word to mean "dwelling in the day" or "dwelling in the night."

The Seasons and Moons of the Cherokee

du no lv ta ni   January
Month of the Cold Moon

ka ga li   February
Month of the Bony Moon

a nu yi   March
Month of the Windy Moon

ka wa ni   April
Month of the Flower Moon

a na a gv ti   May
Month of the Planting Moon

de ha lu yi   June
Month of the Green Corn Moon

gu ye quo ni   July
Month of the Ripe Corn Moon

ga lo nii   August
Month of the End of the Fruit Moon

du li i s di   September
Month of the Nut Moon

du ni nv di   October
Month of the Harvest Moon

nu da de qua   November
Month of the Trading Moon

v s gi ga   December
Month of the Snow Moon

Further Changes

During the relatively peaceful time of the early 1800s, palisades gradually disappeared from Cherokee villages. More and more, European settlers influenced Cherokee members. This led the Cherokee to modify their farming techniques and adopt new ways of building structures. Before long, council houses were no longer built, and traditional homes were replaced by log cabins. Outbuildings, including corn cribs, smokehouses, root cellars, and small barns, were also modeled after those of settlers. Communities became more scattered throughout the mountains, then were replaced altogether by isolated farmsteads. These small farms had large vegetable gardens and cornfields of 5 to 20 acres (2 to 8 hectares). Men began to tend crops and raise horses, pigs, cattle, and other livestock. Before long, however, the Cherokee began to quarrel among themselves about whether to adopt white practices or keep their own culture. It was clear that incorporating European traditions challenged and changed many customs of the Cherokee people.

Of utmost importance to them was the ability to stay on their lands and to control those lands. In 1827, the Cherokee declared themselves a sovereign nation, but the state of Georgia would not recognize this claim. When they took matters to the Supreme Court, the court ruled in favor of Georgia, saying the Cherokee were merely tenants living on the land. This angered many. In 1831, the Cherokee again appeared in the Supreme Court. This time, they addressed the concern that white settlers were living on Cherokee land without a license to do so. The Supreme Court ruled in the Cherokee's favor, but Georgia refused to uphold this decision. To make matters worse, President Andrew Jackson agreed with Georgia and refused to enforce the Supreme Court's outcome.

One year earlier, in 1830, President Andrew Jackson had signed into law the Indian Removal Act. This act gave land in Oklahoma and other parts of the Western Territory—collectively referred to then as Indian Territory—to any tribe east of the Mississippi willing to relocate. While some tribes accepted the offer, most resisted. Those tribes that refused to move were forcibly driven from their homeland. The Cherokee was one such nation. When the act was signed, Cherokee members argued about whether or not to move to Oklahoma. During these years, the town of New Echota, Georgia, became the capital of the Cherokee Nation.

President Andrew Jackson made life difficult for the Cherokee and other Native American communities.

As a soldier, Jackson had been known as a great fighter of Native Americans, and many Cherokee had fought with him against other tribes. As president, Jackson had told the Cherokee they would be able to keep their land if they had fought with him, but the treaty in 1830 carried a different message. The Cherokee felt betrayed. In 1835, a new treaty specifically targeting the Cherokee was drafted and signed by

The People and Culture of the Cherokee

This famous painting shows the Cherokee moving toward a new home in Oklahoma on the Trail of Tears.

members of the Cherokee Nation. In exchange for giving up their land, the Cherokee would receive $5 million. This was called the Treaty of New Echota. However, the majority of Cherokee did not agree with the signing of this treaty. Nevertheless, the US government took this as permission to relocate the tribe. Upon signing the Treaty of New Echota, Major Ridge, a Cherokee chief who negotiated the treaty of removal, said, "I have signed my death warrant."

The Journey of Sorrow

Despite protests and a letter from Chief John Ross to the Senate and the House of Representatives, and the opposition to removal by fifteen thousand Cherokee, the treaty held. In 1838, sixteen thousand Cherokee were forced to give up their ancestral lands. Private John G. Burnett, who served as an interpreter in the removal, wrote, "I saw the helpless Cherokee arrested and dragged from their homes, and driven at the bayonet point into the stockades. And in the chill of a drizzling rain on an October morning I saw them loaded like cattle or sheep into six hundred and forty-five wagons and started toward the west."

Burnett vividly recalled, "On the morning of November the 17th, we encountered a terrific sleet and snow storm with freezing temperatures, and from that day until we reached the end of the fateful journey on March the 26th, 1839, the sufferings of the Cherokee were awful. The trail of the exiles was a trail of death. They had to sleep in the wagons and on the ground without fire. And I have known as many as twenty-two of them to die in one night of pneumonia due to ill treatment, cold, and exposure."

The Trail of Tears became a 700-mile (1,127-kilometer) journey "with four thousand silent graves reaching from the foothills of the Smoky Mountains to what is known as Indian Territory in the West." Women, children, and men died, including the wife of Chief John Ross. Many Native American tribes suffered the loss of their land and forcible relocation, and the Cherokee Trail of Tears has come to symbolize the displacement of all Native Americans, just as the tragic Sioux defeat at Wounded Knee represents all massacres.

During this tragic journey, a story was born. According to the legend of the Cherokee Rose, God, looking down from heaven, decided to honor the brave Cherokees. So, as the blood of the warriors and the tears of the women splashed onto the ground, he changed each drop into a beautiful flower—the

Cherokee Rose. This is why today the flowers are so plentiful in Oklahoma, at the end of the Trail of Tears. The state flower of Georgia, once the Cherokee ancestral home, is also the Cherokee Rose.

Rebuilding a Community

Those men, women, and children who survived the Trail of Tears and arrived at the end of the long journey found a new home in what is now the northeast corner of Oklahoma. Upon arrival, there were other Cherokee groups living in the area. Among them were the members of the Cherokee, now known as the Old Settlers, who had arrived in Indian Territory of their own choosing, rather than being forcibly removed, and members of the party who had signed the Treaty of New Echota. Despite belonging to the same nation, the groups of people gathered on the land, called a reservation, did not always get along.

The Cherokee who had opposed removal were the largest group. They formed a national party, which excluded the others. Some members of the party tried to resolve the conflicts among the Cherokee, but those who had opposed the treaty were so angry at the loss of their homeland that they murdered three members of the national party, including Major Ridge. In the aftermath, hostilities deepened, but by 1846, John Ross, Stand Watie, and other leaders were able to unify the different Cherokee groups and start to build a new nation.

Despite the hardships the Cherokee faced, they continue to hold a place in Native American and North American history. They are a resilient people who do not give up regardless of hardships they must overcome.

Today, storytelling remains an important part of educating future generations.

CHAPTER SIX

I'm proud of being part Cherokee, and I think it's time all us Indians felt the same way.

—Loretta Lynn, country music singer

THE NATION'S PRESENCE NOW

Today, many of the Cherokee live in Oklahoma, Arkansas, or the surrounding area. The three federally recognized Cherokee tribes are the Keetoowah, the Eastern Cherokee, and the Cherokee Nation in Oklahoma. The Cherokee Nation and the Keetoowah both have their headquarters in Tahlequah, Oklahoma. However, the Eastern

Cherokee still live east of the Mississippi, in North Carolina. They all are connected by a shared history, language, customs, traditions, and beliefs.

Upon first arriving in Indian Territory in the 1840s, however, the ancestors of the Georgia Cherokee did not always see eye to eye with their Cherokee brethren already living west of the Mississippi. The groups eventually worked together to bring changes to the Cherokee Nation, and to benefit the members as a whole. Today, the Cherokee comprise one of the largest groups of Native Americans in the United States. Many live in Cherokee County, their own sovereign nation, and not on a reservation. They take great pride in their history and their heritage.

The Keetoowah Band

One of the groups already living in Indian Territory prior to the forced removal along the Trail of Tears was the Keetoowah, or the Kituwah, Band of Native Americans. They are also known as the Old Settlers. Although the Keetoowah originally dwelled in the Cherokee territory of Georgia, Tennessee, Alabama, and the Carolinas, according to the Keetoowah Band's history: "Archaeologists say that Keetoowah/Cherokee families began migrating to a new home in Arkansas by the late 1790s." In the early 1800s, European and American settlers wanted Keetoowah land in the east. In 1817, the Keetoowah signed the Treaty of 1817. In exchange for eastern lands, the Keetoowah were granted land in present-day western Arkansas and northeastern Oklahoma. However, soon after, this land also came under threat. By 1828, many of the Keetoowah had moved farther west, into Indian Territory. By the time the Cherokee tribes travelling the Trail of Tears arrived, the Old Settlers had formed a community of their own. Today, the Keetoowah still exist. Their descendants have established their presence in many ways, including online. To learn more about them, visit: www.keetoowahcherokee.org.

The Eastern Cherokee

Back in the southern Appalachian Mountains, the farms that the Cherokee had left behind were taken over by settlers. The Cherokee had never locked their doors. They had practiced rituals with tobacco or wood that had been struck by lightning to protect their homes from evil spirits—but this hardly stopped the settlers. Many of the settlers moved right into Cherokee cabins, some of which are still occupied today. Cherokee paths through the mountains and valleys became wagon roads for settlers, and eventually the highway systems that now cut across the land.

Not all Cherokee followed the Trail of Tears during the 1838 removal, though. Some fled into the mountains, where they eluded the soldiers in the thick foliage and shadows. The Cherokee had a spell said to make themselves invisible to enemies: "The wind will take me away, and no one but I alone will know it. Trees! Trees! Trees! Trees! It will be swaying them, and they will be with me." Or, "I will pretend to be a leaf from a tree: people will see me, but they will carelessly step over me."

Despite their escape from a harsh and difficult journey, for many years these people struggled to

Cherokee men and women still create beautiful works of art and clothing.

survive. They could not own land, and they were not considered citizens. Over time, with the help of Colonel Will Thomas—a settler who became a good friend of the Cherokee and an adopted member of the tribe— they quietly bought lands that were held in his name. These people were considered outlaws on their own land until 1870, when the federal government at long last recognized their claims. With difficulty, they were able to establish title to the lands that were held in Thomas's name.

Today they are known as the Eastern Cherokee. They now live on a reservation called the Qualla Boundary in North Carolina. The largest Native reservation in

The People and Culture of the Cherokee

the South, the reservation was formally established in 1889. Many people think "Qualla" is a Cherokee word. Actually, the reservation of the Eastern Band of the Cherokee came to be called Qualla Boundary because an old Native woman, whose English name was Polly, lived near Thomas's trading post on Shoal Creek in Cherokee, North Carolina. Because there is no *p* sound in their language, the Cherokee called her "Qualla," and the Qualla Post Office came to be established at the trading post. When Will Thomas acquired the land for the Eastern Cherokee, it was called the Qualla Boundary.

Today, the Eastern Band of the Cherokee maintains its own council house and government on the Cherokee lands at the edge of the Great Smoky Mountains in western North Carolina. The reservation sits on more than 56,000 acres (22,662 ha). The Cherokee have sovereignty over their land and the members of their

This sign is written in Cherokee and English.

tribe; they form their own nation. They operate their own schools, have their own police force, and make their own laws. They hold elections in which tribal leaders campaign for office. At last count, there were over thirteen thousand enrolled members of the Eastern Band. The tribe also has an online presence. To learn more about them, visit: www.nc-cherokee.com.

Regrouping

Upon arriving in Indian Territory, the Cherokee established a newspaper called the *Cherokee Advocate*, which published news, editorials, and advertisements in both Cherokee and English. This helped to inspire the dislocated people. The Cherokee also set up their own schools, and with a new capital city at Tahlequah, Oklahoma, they worked hard to maintain their identity as Native people.

Just as the Cherokee were making a new home for themselves, the Civil War was declared. Many of the Cherokee were slaveholders, and as such, they supported the Confederacy. Their territory became a battleground, and by the end of the war, they were once again devastated. In 1866, the Cherokee were admitted back into the United States when they agreed to free their slaves, allow the Delaware and Shawnee tribes into their Nation, and permit railroad companies to lay tracks across their land.

Over the years, the Cherokee further suffered from a lack of good leadership. Their leaders, selected by the United States president, seldom represented the best interests of the Cherokee people. Many groups of Cherokee disliked this and showed their displeasure

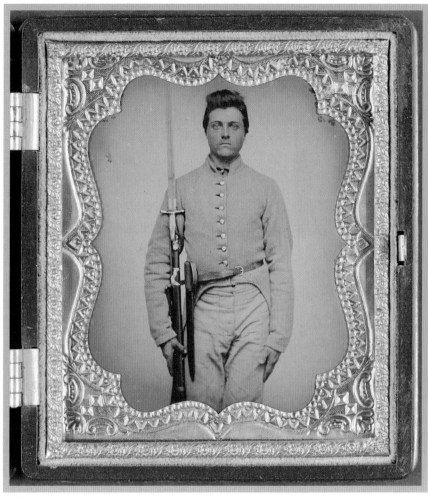

Cherokee soldiers fought in the Civil War, usually on the side of the South.

outwardly. For instance, in protest, the Keetoowah Band retreated into the hills to follow the traditional Cherokee way of life, just as the Eastern Cherokee had struggled against European influences a century before.

In 1889, a commission was formed to abolish the Cherokee reservation and open the territory to non-Native settlement. The land held by the Cherokee was to be divided into plots called allotments. The government sold the surplus land to settlers. Many Cherokee, unfamiliar with business practices, were cheated out of their small allotments. In 1907, the Cherokee were allowed to become United States citizens, but they lost the right to their own government and much of their land.

The Cherokee Nation

Much of the traditional culture has been kept alive in the Cherokee Nation in Oklahoma. Most Cherokee speak English, but their language is taught at home and in school, along with Sequoyah's syllabary. Members of clans live near each other in communities scattered throughout the reservation. Native foods, including chestnut bread, bean bread, and bean dumplings, are served in Cherokee homes. Following the old customs, the Cherokee sing and tell stories. Young people favor jeans and T-shirts, but old women still wear long skirts and bright kerchiefs. They have their own newspaper, *Cherokee One Feather*, which reports on high school cross-country meets and prizes at the county fair, along with information about traditional arts, crafts, and upcoming events.

Today, many Cherokee are also connected to social media. Networks such as Twitter, Facebook, Instagram, and Snapchat are popular online communities that individuals and businesses use and enjoy. Many newspapers, including *Cherokee One Feather*, have an online presence and their own website, complete with an active Twitter feed and discussion boards. Technological companies are also making their mark

Today, the Cherokee language is available on Microsoft Windows and other areas online.

in industry and Cherokee history. In 2015, *Washington Technology* recognized Cherokee Nation Technology Solutions as a Top 8(a) company.

Over the decades, as Cherokee become more connected to modern technology, such as TV, the Internet, and social media, the Cherokee language runs the risk of dying out. So many people—especially young people—are exposed to English through different media every day, and many struggle to use the Cherokee language as they grow. To combat this and to preserve the language, in 2001, a Cherokee immersion school was created in Tahlequah, Oklahoma. This ensures children become completely exposed to the language and can help pass it on to others. As of 2013–2014, there were as many as ninety students enrolled in the school. Likewise, the Cherokee Nation partnered with Microsoft's Local Language Program in the early 2000s. This program ensured that the Cherokee language was accessible across Microsoft platforms. Fluent Cherokee speakers worked with Microsoft to adapt their written language to a computer screen. As a result, in 2014, the Cherokee language was officially included as part of Microsoft Windows 8.

Ceremonies and Celebrations

From April to October the Cherokee hold many public ceremonies, notably "Unto These Hills," a dramatic interpretation of their life. Other ceremonies include powwows and pageants. These events help to strengthen their identity as a people and introduce visitors to Cherokee history. With their population growing, the Eastern Cherokee have come to rely on tourism to support themselves. They have a strong tribal government through which they keep the traditions of their ancestors alive.

One popular tourist attraction has been drawing people in since the 1960s. Diligwa is a historical village that replicates a typical 1700s Cherokee village. It became a tourist attraction in the 1960s and has

A tour guide explains the history of the Cherokee at the Cherokee Heritage Center.

educated others about the Cherokee's past since. In 2013, Diligwa was remodeled to more closely resemble an ancient Cherokee village. Today it remains a popular tourist attraction in Tahlequah, Oklahoma, drawing hundreds of visitors each year.

Continuing the Tribe

The Cherokee have struggled for survival through the twentieth and twenty-first centuries. At one time it was thought that Native Americans, including the Cherokee, were destined for extinction. During the Great Depression of the 1930s, President Franklin D.

Roosevelt introduced many programs as part of the New Deal to help the American people, including the Cherokee. In 1933, he appointed John Collier as commissioner of Native American affairs. Through the Indian Reorganization Act, money was set aside to purchase land for Native people. Although this law did little to help the Cherokee directly, John Collier helped to restore the nation's respect for Native Americans. Some thirty years later, the Cherokee Nation was awarded $15 million in a lawsuit against the federal government because the United States had forced them to sell their land in 1893. They used this money to purchase land and to build a cultural center.

In 1970, the Cherokee Nation regained the right to elect their own leaders. In 1975, they adopted a new constitution, which helped to strengthen the Cherokee Nation. Today, the Cherokee are thriving in Oklahoma. Many live near the historic capital at Tahlequah, as well as in the region around Sallisaw, Oklahoma, where Sequoyah made his home.

The Cherokee Nation maintains an online presence. Their website, www.cherokee.org, is a compelling source of information about the tribe's history, beliefs, and activities today.

Establishing a Future

Today, there are over 350,000 descendants of the Cherokee living throughout the United States. Although they lost most of their ancestral homeland, the spirit of the Cherokee remains very much alive. N. Scott Momaday, an author of Kiowa-Cherokee descent, expresses their deep attachment to the earth and its creations: "Once in his life a man ought to concentrate his mind upon the remembered earth, I believe. He ought to give himself up to a particular landscape in his experience, to look at it from as many angles as he can, to wonder about it, to dwell upon it. He ought to imagine that he touches it with his hands at every season and listens to the sounds that are made upon it. He ought to imagine the creatures there and all the faintest motions of the wind. He ought to recollect the glare of noon and all the colors of the dawn and dusk."

Throughout history, the Cherokee have endured many obstacles and hard times. However, through it all, they have remained unwavering. Their survival has ensured that the Cherokee tribes continue into the present day, and provides hope that they will continue for many years to come.

The Cherokee Nation continues with future generations.

CHAPTER SEVEN

FACES OF THE CHEROKEE NATION

The Cherokee Nation has seen many notable men and women throughout its history. Each has added to the Cherokee's story while making a name for themselves. Here is a list of notable men and women from the Cherokee tribe.

Bloody Fellow (active in late 1700s), also known as Iskagua and Clear Sky, was a leader of the Chickamauga Cherokee of eastern Tennessee. Armed and supplied by the British, he and Dragging Canoe raided American settlements during and after the Revolutionary War. In 1791, he engaged in peace talks with President George Washington in Philadelphia, then the nation's capital, but continued his raids, playing the Spanish against the Americans. He finally signed the Treaty of Tellicoo Blockhouse in 1794 and ended hostilities toward settlers in the southeast.

Elias Boudinot (ca. 1803–1839), also called Galegina, Buck Watie, and Stag Watie, was the first editor of the *Cherokee Phoenix* newspaper. Brother of Stand Watie, nephew of Major Ridge, and cousin of John Ridge, he was among the group that traveled to Washington, DC, to speak with President Andrew Jackson about the removal of the Cherokee from their homeland. An early opponent of removal, he eventually joined the Treaty Party. "I have come to the unpleasant and disagreeable conclusion that our lands, or a large portion of them, are about to be seized and taken from us," he said in an address to Congress. Helping to negotiate the Treaty of New Echota, he was assassinated on the same day as his uncle, Major Ridge.

Bowl (1756–1839), also known as Colonel Bowles, was named after the bowl *diwali* that holds the "black drink" used in Cherokee rituals. Siding with the British in the American Revolution, he fought with the Chickamauga under Dragging Canoe. In 1794, he led a raid against a settlement on the Tennessee River in present-day Alabama. When the Cherokee council denounced his action, known as the Massacre of Muscle Shoals, he and his followers fled across the Mississippi River and settled in Arkansas, later moving to Texas. Bowl became a lieutenant colonel in the Mexican army, but when Texas won independence from Mexico, he had to negotiate another treaty to keep his people's land. However, the treaty was never ratified by the Texas senate, and troops were sent to remove the Cherokee. When the Cherokee refused to leave, they were attacked. Bowl was killed in this massacre and was found clutching a metal box that held the 1836 treaty.

Dennis Wolf Bushyhead (Unaduti) (1826–1898) was the son of a Presbyterian minister. He attended mission schools in the East and in 1841 was a member of a Cherokee delegation to Washington. In 1844, he entered Princeton University but had to return to Oklahoma to take over his deceased father's business interests. In 1848, he became clerk of the Cherokee National Committee, but the next year he headed for California, where he hoped to make a fortune in the gold rush. He stayed for twenty yearas before settling in Tahlequah. In 1871, he became treasurer of the Cherokee Nation in Oklahoma, and in 1879 he was made principal chief. During his two terms as chief (1879–1887), he urged compromise between the traditionalist full-bloods, notably the militant Keetoowah Society, and the mixed-bloods, who favored assimilation. He encouraged the education of his people and economic development through the leasing of land for railroads, logging, mining, and cattle grazing. A staunch supporter of the General Allotment Act, he died in 1898, just a few years before Oklahoma became a state.

Dragging Canoe (Tsiyu-Gunsini) (ca. 1730–1792), the son of the peace chief Attakullakulla and a cousin of Nancy Ward, was born at Running Water Village, or Natchez Town, along the Tennessee River. As a leader, he violently opposed white settlement, refusing to sign the Treaty of Sycamore Shoals in 1775, which ceded much of the land that is now Kentucky and northern Tennessee. Accepting arms from the British, he attacked Appalachian settlements. In 1777, Cherokee leaders relinquished vast stretches of Cherokee land, but Dragging Canoe continued to attack settlers for the next five years. Frontier militias responded by attacking the Chickamauga Cherokee until all their villages were destroyed. In 1782, Dragging Canoe led his followers downriver to present-day Chickamauga, Tennessee, and established the Chickamauga Lower Towns, including his new home Mialaquo. When these towns were destroyed, Dragging Canoe finally sought peace. In 1785, the Treaty of Hopewell established formal borders for Cherokee land, but the US government refused to enforce the treaty. Dragging Canoe responded by attacking squatters, but the Cherokee were forced to cede more land. To the moment of his death in 1791, Dragging Canoe resisted the invasion of his homeland.

Stephen Foreman (1807–1881) was born in Rome, Georgia, one of twelve children of a Scottish trader and a Cherokee mother. After his father died, Foreman moved with his family to Cleveland, Tennessee, where he was educated at a missionary school. He went on to study at the College of Richmond and the Princeton Theological Seminary.

A missionary and educator, Foreman worked on a translation of the Bible into the Cherokee language. He was also an associate editor of the *Cherokee Phoenix* and the *Cherokee Advocate*. Because of his opposition to removal he was briefly imprisoned in 1838, then forced to march on the Trail of Tears. Settling in Indian Territory, Foreman continued to serve as a leader, helping to organize a public school system and becoming its first superintendent. In 1844, he was elected to the supreme court of the Cherokee Nation, and he served as executive councilor from 1847 to 1855. During the Civil War he remained neutral, preferring to work as a missionary in Texas. He returned to Indian Territory after the war and started a church in the former home of Elias Boudinot.

Junaluska (ca. 1795–1858), siding with the United States in the Creek War of 1813–1814, led a group of Cherokee warriors against the Red Stick Creeks. In 1814, at the Battle of Horseshoe Bend, he is believed to have killed a Creek warrior who was about to tomahawk General Andrew Jackson. Junaluska and his warriors swam across the Tallapoosa River and charged the Creek forces in the rear. Through this bold move he was able to save the Americans. He reputedly acquired his name, which means "He Who Tries Repeatedly But Fails," because he swore he would annihilate the Creek during this war. He went on the Trail of Tears, but eventually returned to North Carolina. As a reward for his service to the United States, he was given a large tract of land.

William Keeler (1908–1987), president of Phillips Petroleum Company and principal chief of the Cherokee Nation, once said, "Forgive the past and remove resentment from your hearts. Even the strongest person cannot carry such a burden for long."

George Lowry (active in 1820s–1830s), whose Cherokee name Agili means "He Is Rising," was one of the leaders who agreed to surrender one-third of the remaining Eastern Cherokee lands in 1817. In exchange, the Cherokee people were to receive a tract of land of equal size between the Arkansas and White Rivers. In this treaty, relocation to the West was also voluntary. After the forced removal on the Trail of Tears, Lowry became chief of council of the emigrants who formed the new Cherokee government west of the Mississippi.

John Lowry (active in early 1800s) led four hundred Cherokee warriors in support of General Andrew Jackson against the Red Stick Creeks in 1813–1814. As an ally of the United States, Lowry helped to take the village of Hillabee, Alabama. He also fought in the Battle of Horseshoe Bend, his warriors swimming the Tallapoosa River and attacking the Creeks from the rear.

Wilma Mankiller (1945–2010) was born in the Indian Hospital at Tahlequah, Oklahoma, and spent her early childhood in Rocky Mountain, Oklahoma. She was the sixth of eleven children. At age eleven, her family moved to San Francisco, California, in a relocation program sponsored by the Bureau of Indian Affairs. However, her father was able to get only low-paying jobs that barely supported the large family. Despite these hardships, Mankiller was not aware of her family's poverty until later in life.

Wilma Mankiller

During the 1960s and 1970s, Mankiller was active in community programs in San Francisco. After earning her master's degree, she returned to Oklahoma in 1979. That same year, she survived a head-on car crash, resulting in many injuries requiring multiple surgeries and years of rehabilitation. Four years later, she was elected the first woman deputy chief of the Cherokee Nation. In 1985, she was the first woman to be elected chief of the Cherokee Nation. She assumed the position when her predecessor resigned, and she was later re-elected. Her time as chief ended in 1995; however, while she was chief the Cherokee Nation's population more than doubled, from 68,000 to 170,000. In

1998, President Bill Clinton bestowed upon her the Presidential Medal of Freedom. Up until her death she remained an advisor and prominent member of the Cherokee Nation. She died from pancreatic cancer in 2010 at the age of sixty-four.

Oconostota (ca. 1710–1785), whose name means "Groundhog Sausage," was a member of the Cherokee delegation that met King George II in England in 1730. War chief of the Cherokee during the 1750s, he fought against the settlers who were pushing into the mountains. In 1760, he started the Cherokee War when he led a Cherokee war party against Fort Prince George, South Carolina. It required two armies to defeat Oconostota, and afterward he and his warriors continued to fight from hideouts in the mountains. In 1763, after many villages were destroyed, he finally signed a peace treaty that ceded large portions of Cherokee lands. During the Revolutionary War, Oconostota sided with his old enemies, the British, against the Americans. Once again, the Cherokee saw their villages attacked and destroyed. Oconostota died in 1783 shortly after turning the leadership of his band over to his son Tuksi.

John Ridge (1803–1839) was the son of Major Ridge and cousin of Elias Boudinot and Stand Watie. He was also known as Ganun'dalegi, which means "One Who Follows the Ridge." Born in Rome, Georgia, he attended the Cornwall Foreign Mission School in Connecticut, where he met his future wife, Sarah Bird Northrup. Returning to Georgia with his bride, Ridge became an important tribal leader. He wrote articles for the *Cherokee Phoenix* and served as interpreter and secretary for several tribal delegations to Washington, DC. A member of the Treaty Party, which considered removal to be inevitable, he signed the Treaty of New Echota in 1835. Ridge wrote to Andrew Jackson in 1836 to protest the cruel treatment of the Cherokee people by the citizens of Georgia. After he was forced to march on the Trail of Tears, Ridge was murdered with his father and Elias Boudinot by people who resented their signing of the removal treaty.

Major Ridge (1771–1839), known as Nunna Hidihi, meaning "Man of the Mountaintop," was elected to the Cherokee Council when he was just twenty-one. He eventually became speaker because of his skill as an orator. He received the name "Major" during the Creek War (1813–1814) in which he served with General Andrew Jackson. He was one of the leaders of the Treaty Party who negotiated the agreement that relinquished Cherokee homelands. Although he was considered a traitor by many of his own people, he felt that he had no choice and that his actions saved many lives. After relocation in Indian Territory, he was killed by opponents of the Treaty of New Echota in 1839.

Will Rogers (1879–1935), the popular "cowboy philosopher" and humorist on radio, screen, and the stage, also wrote his own newspaper column. He often referred to Native Americans in his comments, once saying, "My ancestors did not come over on the Mayflower—they met the boat."

John Ross (1790–1866) was born along the Coosa River in Georgia to a Scottish father and a mother who was part Cherokee and part Scottish. Although raised among the Cherokee, Ross was educated at home by tutors of European ancestry and attended the academy at Kingston, Tennessee. Like many other Cherokee, he participated in the Creek War (1813–1814) as an ally of General Andrew Jackson. When he was twenty-three, he married Quatie, a nearly full-blooded Cherokee.

Chief John Ross

In 1814, he established Ross's Landing, a trading post and ferry on the Tennessee River at the site of present-day Chattanooga. Active in Cherokee affairs, Ross participated in a Cherokee delegation to Washington, DC, in 1816. Two years later, he returned to the US capital and negotiated the Cherokee Treaty. He also drafted the response to federal demands that the Cherokee exchange their lands for tracts of land west of the Mississippi River.

In the 1820s, after the Cherokee had established a republican form of government modeled after the United States, Ross advocated education and Christianity in hopes that the Cherokee would be able to govern themselves independently in their own state. He helped establish New Echota, Georgia, as the national capital and moved his family there. The Cherokee adopted a constitution, as well as a senate and house of representatives, and Ross was elected principal chief in 1828.

Between 1828 and 1831, the state of Georgia stripped the Cherokee of many of their rights, and from 1830 to 1838, Ross led many delegations to Washington to argue on behalf of his people. Yet like so many other Cherokee, Ross was forced to leave his home and march on the Trail of Tears. His wife, Quatie, died on the arduous journey. Upon their arrival in Indian Territory, Ross, Sequoyah, and other peacemakers sought to reunite the Cherokee people. Ross helped write the new constitution and was elected principal chief in 1839. During the Civil War, he sought neutrality, but the Cherokee became even more divided over the question of slavery. For the rest of his life, Ross worked as a leader of his faction of the Cherokee people.

Sequoyah (ca. 1770–1843), also known as George Gist, devised a unique alphabet for the Cherokee. His name is derived from the Cherokee word *sikwaji* or *sogwili*, meaning "sparrow" or "principal bird." Growing up with his mother near Willstown, Alabama, as a boy Sequoyah tended dairy cattle and made cheese. He broke horses, raised corn, and became a good trader. A hunter and trapper, he was crippled in an accident. Forced to give up his active life, he became an accomplished silversmith.

He married Sarah (Sally) in 1815, after serving with Andrew Jackson in the Creek War (1813–1814). Three years later, he moved his family to Arkansas with Chief Jolly's band. He had already begun his syllabary in 1809 and finally completed the monumental project in 1821. Based on eighty-five characters, the method of writing was formally adopted by the Cherokee National Council, and the syllabary became widely used in publications, including the weekly newspaper, the *Cherokee Phoenix*.

Sequoyah moved with his wife and children to Indian Territory in 1829, where he worked to unite the factions among the Cherokee people. He was the first member of any Native American tribe to be granted a pension. He died while searching for a lost tribe of Cherokee reported to be living in Mexico. About his syllabary, which he called "talking leaves," he said, "I thought that if I could make certain things fast on paper, it would be like catching a wild animal and taming it."

Nimrod Jarrett Smith (ca. 1838–1893) was born near present-day Murphy, North Carolina. During the Civil War, he served as a sergeant in the Confederate army in an Eastern Cherokee company under the command of Colonel W. H. Thomas, a Cherokee trader. Married to Mary Guthrie, a woman of European descent, he became the first elected principal chief of the Eastern Cherokee in the 1870s and held the position until his death in 1893. Under his leadership, the Eastern Cherokee regained title to their lands in North Carolina. Smith also created a modern educational system for his people.

Redbird Smith (1850–1918) was born near Fort Smith, Arkansas. As Smith grew up, his family supported the Keetoowah Society, which worked to preserve Cherokee heritage and to protect Cherokees against settlers eager for their land. After the Civil War, the Keetoowah Society became less important because there were no major land disputes threatening the Native people. However, the General Allotment Act of 1887 called for the elimination of tribal land held in common, with 160-acre (65 ha) parcels given to individual members. A principal chief and Cherokee traditionalist, Smith revived the Keetoowah Society and fought against allotment and Oklahoma statehood. He feared that speculators would cheat individuals out of their land and the Cherokee would lose their identity as a people. He lobbied Congress and encouraged Cherokee people not to enroll in the census of 1900. In 1902, Smith was arrested and forced to enroll in the census and accept allotment. In 1905, under protest, the Cherokee became the last people in Indian Territory to agree to allotment. Two years later, Oklahoma became a state, and many of Smith's followers moved to the Cookson Hills in northeastern Oklahoma to preserve their traditional way of life. In 1908, Smith was elected principal chief of the Cherokee. In 1912, he joined with Creek, Choctaw, and Chickasaw leaders to form the Four Mothers Society, leading the political and legal battle to restore tribal and cultural heritage.

Tahchee (ca. 1790–1850) was born in Turkey Town on the Coosa River in present-day Alabama. He later moved with his family to Arkansas, where Bowl had settled with his band of Cherokee. Raised to be a plains hunter and warrior, as a young man, Tahchee participated in raids on the Osage. Enraged at the 1828 treaty between the Cherokee and the United States, Tahchee crossed the Red River into Texas and attacked the Osage and the Comanche tribes. Declared an outlaw by the US Army, with a $500 reward on his head, Tahchee became a famous renegade on the Great Plains.

For years he raided trading posts and Native camps, then made his peace with the United States and became an army scout working against the Comanche. He also hunted to provide game for the army. In his later years, he settled down as a farmer along the Canadian River near Fort Gibson in Oklahoma.

Tsali (died 1838) lived as a farmer and hunter with his family in Valley Town in the Great Smoky Mountains of North Carolina. In the spring of 1838, soldiers came to arrest Tsali and his family and take them to the stockade to await their departure on the Trail of Tears. On the way, his wife stumbled and the soldiers goaded her with their bayonets, which angered Tsali. Speaking in Cherokee, he told his sons and brothers-in-law to be ready when he feigned an injury. Shortly afterward, he pretended to hurt his ankle, and when one of the soldiers approached him, he attacked him. One of his sons, Ridges, and his brother-in-law, Lowney, jumped the other soldier. The first soldier was killed by his own gun and the other fled into the woods.

That summer, Tsali and his family hid in a cave on Clingman's Dome, a high peak in the Great Smoky Mountains. They were joined by three hundred other Cherokee who opposed removal. In the fall, General

Winfield Scott sent word through Will Thomas, an adopted Cherokee, that if those responsible for the death of the soldier surrendered, his troops would cease their search for the other fugitives. Tsali, Lowney, and Ridges gave themselves up and, following a military trial, were executed by firing squad. Tsali is now honored as a hero among the Eastern Cherokee.

James Wafford (1806–1896) was born near present-day Clarkesville, Georgia, the grandson of a colonel in the Revolutionary War. His grandfather established Wafford Settlement in 1785 on Cherokee lands, and about 100 acres (40 ha) were ceded by the tribe in 1804. A cousin of Sequoyah, Wafford's mother was of Cherokee, Natchez, and European ancestry. Also known as Tsuskwanunnawata, meaning "Worn-out Blanket," Wafford attended a mission school at Valleytown, where he worked on a translation of a Sunday school speller. In 1824, he worked for the Census Bureau, gaining valuable knowledge about the Cherokee people and their homeland. During the Trail of Tears, he served as a commander of a group of emigrants and later became a member of the Cherokee Nation tribal council. In 1891, James Mooney interviewed him at Tahlequah in Indian Territory for his monumental study of the Cherokee.

Nancy Ward (ca. 1738–1824) was born into the Wolf Clan at Chota, the old Cherokee capital near Fort Loudon, Tennessee. Also known as Tsiistunagiska, or "Wild Rose," because of her rosy complexion, and Nanye-hi, or "One Who Goes About," she was a sister of Attakullakulla and a cousin of renowned war chief

A Cherokee gravesite.

Dragging Canoe. While still a teenager she married Kingfisher, a Cherokee of the Deer clan, and had two children with him.

At the Battle of Taliwa against the Creeks, she helped her husband, and when he died in battle, she took up his musket. For her bravery, she was given the name *ghighau*—beloved woman. She subsequently became head of the Women's Council and voted on the Chief's Council. One of her rights was to pardon condemned captives, and she often spared white captives. She became known as an advocate of peace, and during the American Revolution she warned settlers of impending Cherokee attacks. At the end of the war she advocated reconciliation and friendship. Although many people on both sides of the conflict disagreed with her, there were few who did not respect her.

The People and Culture of the Cherokee

During this time, she married her second husband, an Irish trader, and had three children with him. She opened a thriving inn at Womankiller Ford on the Ocowee River and became known as "Nancy," a version of her Cherokee name, Nanye-hi. As more people of European descent poured into Tennessee, she became disillusioned with her policy of friendship toward settlers and advised the Cherokee Council of 1817 to cede no more lands and to resist removal—a policy she urged until her death in 1824. Among the Cherokee people, she is still honored for her courage, beauty, and wisdom.

Stand Watie (1806–1871) was born in Coosawalee near present-day Rome, Georgia. A member of the Deer clan, he was also known as Degataga, meaning "Standing Together as One," "Stand Firm," or "Immovable." Like his older brother, Elias Boudinot, Watie attended school at Brainerd Mission in eastern Tennessee, then worked with his brother on the *Cherokee Phoenix*. Viewing removal as inevitable, he took an active role in the Treaty Party in opposition to John Ross. Along with his uncle and cousin, Major and John Ridge, Watie signed the Treaty of New Echota in 1835. After the Trail of Tears, he was to be killed along with the Ridges and his brother Elias. However, he was warned, and of the four men he was the only one who managed to escape the murderers. He retaliated by setting fire to the home of John Ross.

Helping to reorganize the Cherokee in Indian Territory, Watie was a member of the council from 1845 to 1861, serving as speaker from 1857 to 1859. During the Civil War, he became a Confederate general, leading two Cherokee Mounted Rifles regiments in more battles west of the Mississippi River than any other fighting unit. In 1864, he was elected principal chief of the southern band of Cherokees and was the last Confederate to put down his arms at the end of the Civil War.

In 1866, he helped to negotiate the Cherokee Reconstruction Treaty, then settled down to farm on the Grand River near Bernice in Indian Territory. He married Sarah Caroline "Betsy" Bell, with whom he had five children. Because of his thorough knowledge of Cherokee culture, he became a source for Henry Rowe Schoolcraft's famous study of Native American life.

White Path (1763–1835) was most likely born near Turniptown near present-day Ellijay, Georgia. During the Revolutionary War, under the command of Chief Dragging Canoe, he raided American settlements. However, in the Creek War of 1813–1814, he sided with the Americans against William Weatherford and the Red Stick Creeks.

Living on a small farm near Turniptown, White Path served on the Cherokee National Council. However, he opposed the assimilation of Native people into American culture, and when he spoke out against the new tribal laws and the work of missionaries among the Cherokee, he was ejected from his council seat in disgrace. In 1827, he and other traditionalists created another council that opposed the Cherokee constitution drafted under the leadership of Chief John Ross. However, within a few months, White Path's rebellion lost momentum, and nontraditional accommodations were added into the Cherokee constitution.

Although he remained an independent spirit, White Path was re-elected to the Cherokee National Council on August 28, 1827.

Yonagusta (ca. 1760–1839), whose name means "Drowning Bear," was a peace chief of the North Carolina Cherokees, widely known for his diplomacy and oratory. His band lived along the Tuckasegee River, but in 1819 moved near the Oconaluftee River. When he was about sixty years old, Yonagusta became so ill that he lapsed into a coma. Believing he was dead, his people began to mourn him, but after a day or so, he revived. Claiming he had visited the spirit world, he became a prophet, denouncing the use of alcohol.

In 1829, Yonagusta and fifty-eight other people left the Cherokee Nation and became citizens of Haywood County, North Carolina. Purchasing a tract of land through Yonagusta's adopted son Will Thomas, who had become an attorney, they managed to avoid removal to Indian Territory.

The Cherokee's history is long and complex, filled with many trials and tribulations. However, today the Cherokee are a sovereign nation, recognized as one of the most enduring tribes of North America. Their people live close to the land and remember their ancestors, encouraging younger generations to remember, too, and be proud of their unique heritage.

CHRONOLOGY

1540 Spanish explorer Hernando de Soto travels through Cherokee country.

1629 The Cherokee begin to trade with English settlers.

1721 Charleston Treaty with the governor of the Carolinas is thought to be first Cherokee concession of land.

1759 Cherokee chiefs are imprisoned by English soldiers.

1776 The Cherokee side with the British in the Revolutionary War.

1785 Treaty of Hopewell is the first agreement between the United States and the Cherokee.

1791 Treaty of Holston calls for "civilization" of the Cherokee by providing farm tools and technical advice.

1802 Thomas Jefferson signs Georgia Compact supporting Native removal.

1817 Treaty provides for land in Arkansas. A group of Cherokee migrate voluntarily and establish government there, but are soon forced to move into Indian Territory.

1821 Sequoyah finishes the Cherokee syllabary which promotes literacy among the Cherokee.

1822 Cherokee supreme court is established.

1824 First written laws of the Cherokee Nation are enacted.

1825 New Echota, Georgia, becomes the Cherokee capital.

1827 Cherokee Nation is established with the passage of a democratic constitution and election of John Ross as chief.

1828 *The Cherokee Phoenix* is published in English and Cherokee.

1828–1830 Georgia legislature abolishes tribal government and claims authority over Cherokee lands.

1832 US Supreme Court supports tribal sovereignty in Worcester v. Georgia, but President Andrew Jackson opposes the decision and Georgia holds a lottery for Cherokee lands.

1835 Cherokee leaders agree to surrender their homeland to the United Stataes in the Treaty of New Echota.

1838–1839 On the Trail of Tears the Cherokee are exiled from their homeland to Indian Territory in present-day Oklahoma.

1844 *The Cherokee Advocate* is established as the first newspaper in Indian Territory.

1846 A seven-year war among the Cherokee in Oklahoma comes to an end.

1851 Cherokee Male and Female Seminaries established. The Female Seminary is the first school for girls west of the Mississippi River.

1859 Original Keetoowah Society is organized in Oklahoma to maintain Cherokee traditions and to fight slavery.

1861 The Cherokee Nation becomes allies of the Confederacy in the Civil War.

1866 Tribal land rights in Oklahoma are limited when the Cherokee are forced to negotiate peace with the United States after the Civil War.

1870 United States recognizes the Cherokee people as American citizens.

1876 The Eastern Cherokee are awarded 50,000 acres (20,234 ha) of Qualla Boundary land in present-day North Carolina.

1887 General Allotment Act requires individual ownership of lands held in common by members of the Cherokee Nation.

1889 Qualla Boundary, the largest reservation in the South, is formally established in North Carolina.

1905 Land allotment begins after an official census of members of the Cherokee Nation is taken.

1907 Oklahoma becomes a state and dissolves Cherokee tribal government.

1934 Indian Reorganization Act establishes a land base for tribes and a legal means for self-government.

1941–1945 Over one thousand Cherokee serve in the United States military during World War II.

1961 The Cherokee Nation is awarded $15 million in a lawsuit against the United States government.

1985 Wilma Mankiller is elected principal chief of the Cherokee Nation in Oklahoma.

1988 Cherokee Nation joins Eastern Band in observing the 150th anniversary of the Trail of Tears.

1990 Wilma Mankiller signs historic self-government agreement in which the Cherokee Nation in Oklahoma assumes responsibility for federal funds formally administered by the Bureau of Indian Affairs.

1994 Wilma Mankiller announces that she will not run for re-election.

1995 Joe Byrd and Garland Eagle elected principal chief and deputy chief.

1999 Chad "Corntassel" Smith becomes principal chief of the Cherokee Nation.

2001 The Cherokee Immersion School opens in Talehquah, Oklahoma.

2011 Bill John Baker takes over as principal chief.

2013 Diligwa is remodeled off archeological plans.

2014 Microsoft's Local Language Program completes work with Cherokee speakers; Cherokee is included as part of Windows 8.

GLOSSARY

Aniyvwiya Cherokee name for themselves, meaning "real people" or "principal people."

Appalachia Mountainous region of the eastern United States, largely in the Upland South.

atayohi Cherokee round dance.

Bering Strait The body of water that separates Russia and Alaska. During the last Ice Age, a land bridge across the strait allowed for migration from one continent to the other.

breechcloth A cloth or skin worn between the legs; also called breechclout.

buckskin Deer hide softened by a tanning or curing process.

clan A group of families related to a common ancestor.

consensus General agreement.

dance ground An open area in which the Cherokee held dances and other important ceremonies; also called square ground.

Great Smoky Mountains A mountain range of the southern Appalachians.

handbreadth Unit of measure from 2.5 to 4 inches (6.35 to 10.16 centimeters).

Iroquoian A language family of eastern North America, including Cherokee and the Iroquois languages of New York and southern Canada.

Kanati Cherokee name for the Great Spirit.

lacrosse Modern sport based on a popular woodland Native ball game.

New Echota Town in Georgia that became the latter-day capital of the Cherokee Nation.

palisade A strong wall of pointed wooden stakes or logs used as a defense.

parched corn Corn that is mixed with wood ashes in a pot or pan and dried over a low fire.

Red chief A military or war leader of the Cherokee.

river cane Cane similar to bamboo that is split into strips used in weaving baskets.

shaman Religious leader with healing powers and a knowledge of medicine.

square ground An open area in which the Cherokee held dances and other important ceremonies; also called dance ground.

tciloki Creek word for the Cherokee meaning "people of a different speech."

uka Chief.

Upland South Southern Appalachian Mountains.

White chief Civil, or peacetime, Cherokee leader also known as the most beloved man.

yûñwi tsunsdi The little people of Cherokee folklore.

BIBLIOGRAPHY

Case, Marc W. *Simple Cherokee: Let's Learn Cherokee Syllabary*. Bloomington, IN: AuthorHouse, 2012.

Confer, Clarissa W. *The Cherokee Nation in the Civil War*. Norman, OK: University of Oklahoma Press, 2012.

Conley, Robert J. *The Cherokee Nation: A History*. Albuquerque, NM: University of New Mexico Press: 2008.

Dunbar-Oritz, Roxanne. *An Indigenous Peoples' History of the United States*. ReVisioning American History. Beacon Press, 2014.

Fox, Pamela Carmelle. *Cherokee Education: Path to Autonomy and Sovereignty*. Bakersfield, CA: Kemama Publishing, 2013.

Hausmann, Blake M. *Riding the Trail of Tears*. Lincoln, NE: University of Nebraska Press, 2011.

Hill, Sarah H. *Weaving New Worlds: Southeastern Cherokee Women and Their Basketry*. Chapel Hill, NC: University of North Carolina Press, 1997.

Howell, D. Bruce. *1806: The Exploration and Settlement of the Cherokee Nation in Indian Territory*. Seattle, WA: CreateSpace, 2015.

Langguth, A. J. *Driven West: Andrew Jackson and the Trail of Tears to the Civil War*. New York: Simon & Schuster, 2010.

Mankiller, Wilma, and Michael Wallis. *Mankiller: A Chief and Her People*. New York: St. Martin's Griffin, 2000.

Perdue, Theda and Michael D. Green. *The Cherokee Nation and the Trail of Tears*. New York: Penguin, 2007.

Rice, Horace R. *The Buffalo Ridge Cherokee: A Remnant of a Great Nation Divided*. Berwyn Heights, MD: Heritage Books, 2009.

Smith, Chad "Corntassel." *Leadership Lessons from the Cherokee Nation: Learn From All I Observe*. New York: McGraw-Hill Education, 2013.

Smithers, Gregory D. *The Cherokee Diaspora: An Indigenous History of Migration, Resettlement, and Identity*. New Haven, CT: Yale University Press, 2015.

Stewart, Mark. *The Indian Removal Act: Forced Relocation*. Snapshots in History. Minneapolis, MN: Compass Point Books, 2007.

FURTHER INFORMATION

Want to know more about the Cherokee Nation? Check out these websites, videos, and organizations.

Websites

Cherokee Nation

www.cherokee.org

This is the official website of the Cherokee Nation. Learn all about the tribe and connect to other social networks, such as YouTube, Facebook, and Twitter.

Unto These Hills

www.visitcherokeenc.com/play/attractions/unto-these-hills-outdoor-drama

This website details the Cherokee's successful living history event "Unto These Hills."

Visit Cherokee North Carolina

www.visitcherokeenc.com

Visit this interactive website to learn more about the Cherokee of North Carolina, including what special events are coming up in the calendar year.

Videos

Cherokee Nation: Helping Save a Language

www.youtube.com/watch?v=ybhnlN-IQI4

This video describes the efforts being taken today to preserve the Cherokee language.

Diligwa, A Living Cherokee History

www.youtube.com/watch?v=Ad0ueTRHlPg

This video takes the viewer on a tour of Diligwa, a replica 1700s Cherokee village.

Excerpt from Voices of North Carolina

www.youtube.com/watch?v=Ecm_DIpocIo

Watch as members of the Cherokee Nation speak in Cherokee and explain the need to continue speaking the language today.

The Trail of Tears

www.youtube.com/watch?v=7LSkfmCj8Jg

Learn about the events leading to the Trail of Tears and the journey that fifteen thousand Cherokee endured in this historical documentary filmed by the National Park Service.

Organizations

Cherokee Heritage Center (Tsa-La-Gi)
PO Box 515
Tahlequah, OK 74465
(918) 456-6007
www.cherokeeheritage.org

Cherokee Nation
PO Box 948
Tahlequah, OK 74465
(918) 453-5000
www.cherokee.org

Cherokee Welcome Center
PO Box 460
Cherokee, NC 28719
(800) 438-1601
www.visitcherokeenc.com

Eastern Band of Cherokee Indians
PO Box 455
Cherokee, NC 28719
(828) 497-7000
www.nc-cherokee.com or www.cherokeesmokies.com

Museum of the Cherokee
589 Tsali Boulevard
Cherokee, NC 28719
(828) 497-3481
www.cherokeemuseum.org

Oconaluftee Indian Village

218 Drama Road

Cherokee, NC 28719

(866) 554-4557

www.cherokeesmokies.com/oconaluftee_village.html

Qualla Arts and Crafts Mutual, Inc.

645 Tsali Boulevard

Cherokee, NC 28719

(828) 497-3103

www.quallaartsandcrafts.com

United Keetoowah Band of Cherokee

PO Box 746

Tahlequah, OK 74465

(918) 431-1818

www.keetoowahcherokee.org

INDEX

Page numbers in **boldface** are illustrations. Entries in **boldface** are glossary terms.

The People and Culture of the Cherokee

ABOUT THE AUTHORS

Cassie M. Lawton is a freelance editor and writer living and working in New York City.

Raymond Bial has published more than eighty books— most of them photography books—during his career. His photo-essays for children include *Corn Belt Harvest, Amish Home, Frontier Home, Shaker Home, The Underground Railroad, Portrait of a Farm Family, With Needle and Thread: A Book About Quilts, Mist Over the Mountains: Appalachia and Its People, Cajun Home,* and *Where Lincoln Walked.*

As with his other work, Bial's deep feeling for his subjects is evident in both the text and illustrations. He travels to tribal cultural centers, photographing homes, artifacts, and surroundings and learning firsthand about the national lifeways of these peoples.

The emeritus director of a small college library in the Midwest, he lives with his wife and three children in Urbana, Illinois.